NINE
ESSENTIAL LAWS
FOR
BECOMING
INFLUENTIAL

Written By:
Dr. Tony Zeiss

Edited by:
Tom & Todd Rutherford

Nine Essential Laws For Becoming Influential

Written By Dr. Tony Zeiss
Edited by Tom and Todd Rutherford

Copyright © 2000 by P. Anthony Zeiss

Library of Congress Cataloging-in-Publication Data
Zeiss, Anthony.

Becoming Influential: / Tony Zeiss.
ISBN 1-929496-01-X

Printed in the United States of America.

Published by:
Triumphant Publishers International
P. O. Box 701350
Tulsa, Oklahoma 74170
(918-) 523-5475

Table of Contents

Preface

You can achieve these Nine Essential Laws for Becoming Influential! The sooner you learn them and use them, the sooner you will find the success you seek. Using these laws will help you in life achievements and will ensure success in every area of your life. But first, a word of warning. You will not be successful using these laws unless you are prepared to take them and use them seriously and consistently.

Most unsuccessful people feel rejected, defeated, cheated, or perplexed. They usually go through an emotional process similar to the stages of grief which include: denial, followed by anger, depression, fear, sometimes guilt, and finally acceptance. These changing emotions are quite normal. Unfortunately, emotions and innermost feelings drive beliefs and shape self-concept. In consequence, what you feel, you believe. And belief drives behavior. If you are depressed or angry when you look for advancement opportunities, your speech, your posture, and all of your nonverbal actions telegraph that depression or anger. That is why you have to work through any negative feelings surrounding your current condition and get on with the positive and successful adventure of experiencing success. Strap on your seat belt, you are already on your way toward becoming influential!

You can use scores of resources to become influential and advance in life. But, your network of social and professional friends will be your best resource. Books, tapes, and seminars can help you learn techniques for increasing your value. But it is up to you—and only you—to sell yourself. In this respect, it's your relationship with others and their perception of your value to them that really matters. To be influential you need to widen the winner's circle by helping others achieve their goals. The Nine Essential Laws presented in this book will guide you in selling yourself successfully to any group and becoming influential.

You can use any number of gimmicks to give yourself an edge in life. Using your unique charm, being in all the right places at the right times, and always agreeing with others can help, but using the nine laws described in this book will be significantly more effective. Ignore any of them and all the flattery and gimmicks in the world will not help. Each law is unique. Learn them, live them, and use them to your advantage.

These nine laws present the primary traits the world wants in people. These nine laws are mostly attitudinal in nature. That is, you can make them a part of your life by believing in them and deciding to use them. You see, positive behavior is essential to life's success.

The formula for a secure and successful life is this: (1) believe in yourself, (2) focus on your life goals, and (3) employ the Nine Essential Laws for Becoming Influential!

Introduction

Can one really become a "necessity" to others? Not so much in the literal sense because we have emerged into a knowledge-based and global economy where change is constant. No one can completely control the variable dimensions of his or her life. However, everyone can significantly enhance his or her security, advancement, and influence by consistently exhibiting those skills and behaviors people most admire. These same skills and behaviors will help you to insure success in life. You may not be totally influential in a specific place setting, but you can become influential in the broader marketplace.

Unfortunately, most people do not realize that they have almost unlimited control over their life and the conditions that affect it. Some people, for instance, develop the misconception that they are inadequate, under-skilled, or discriminated against because of age, race, gender, size, or any number of self-created excuses to protect their fragile egos. This is typical, but self-defeating, behavior. Regardless of your situation, you can and must emphasize your strengths and have the confidence to sell yourself to others.

As the world shifts into a global economy, businesses are moving into a perpetual state of rightsizing. That is, they downsize to become more competitive and upsize as demands for their new products and services increase. Corporate America, and in some cases the public sector, is reengineering to increase its competitive stature by focusing on more efficient processes, greater productivity, and reduced labor costs. In short, America's private and public employers are undergoing a continuous process of job elimination and job creation as a necessary competitive technique. This is a natural process. Consider jobs in agriculture. In 1900, 95 percent of the workforce was in agriculture. Today, less than 2 percent of the workforce is employed in this area. The average worker today will change jobs seven times and careers three times during his or her working years. Through new opportunities created by economic growth, success has never been better!

To survive in our environment, you must understand how to best prepare to sell yourself to others. You can do this by developing a clear life vision, getting the necessary skills, and by undertaking and practicing the traits people seek most in their relationships. Successful people know how to leave the past behind them and look forward to their goal. They know that the best predictor of success is to have a clear goal, a positive expectation to achieve it, and the self-discipline to continuously work toward it.

America has entered the information age. The demand for knowledge-based skills is essential for anyone who aspires to become influential and successful in life. Business leaders are telling us that credentials are still important, but the ability to transform knowledge into performance is the critical factor that determines a person's value. Truett Cathy, founder and CEO of Chick Fil-A restaurants, recently visited Central

Piedmont Community College in Charlotte, North Carolina. While on a campus tour, he addressed two classes of culinary students and offered this advice. "Academic credentials are important and will help you get in the door, but performance and dependability will get you success." Once a goal has been established, the ability to access information, process information, and apply information in your life becomes a critical component of success. In the end, your best opportunity to reach your goals and become influential depends almost entirely upon you and your ability to positively influence others.

With over thirty years of experience helping people learn advancement skills, I have fleshed out the nine attributes that are keys to success in life. I call these acquisition -retention attributes the Nine Essential Laws for Becoming Influential. You will dramatically increase your chances for success by learning and using these laws in your efforts to advance your life goals.

Dr. P. Anthony Zeiss

Chapter One

The Law of Attitude

ENTHUSIASM IS CONTAGIOUS!

The Most Importamt Law For Becoming Influential is Having a Positive Attitude

Yes, the most important attribute for becoming influential is a positive attitude. And guess who has absolute control over your attitude? You are correct! You alone determine how you will face each day, react to each circumstance, and behave toward others. People want to be associated with positive, happy, "Can Do" people.

You can verify the truth of this success trait by answering these questions:

☞ *Do I enjoy being with positive or negative people?*

☞ *Who most often advances, negative or positive people?*

☞ *Do positive or negative people most often reach their goals?*

The answers are obvious. Optimistic, cheerful people are fun to be around and usually do well in their endeavors to succeed in life.

Research indicates that a positive attitude is nearly always at the very top of the list of characteristics people desire in others. Individuals who are happy are

14

most likely to be identified as "rising stars". It's no wonder, then, that the most successful people have positive attitudes.

I can give scores of examples of people who lost altitude on their life flight because of their poor attitudes. These people seem to relish their chronic discontent, and yet they complain when life refuses to promote them. Unfortunately, it is easy to get caught up with the whiners and complainers. Misery likes company and these folks will befriend anyone who joins in with and reinforces their negative beliefs. We become what we think about. In a very short time we can become negative about everything without realizing it. By seeking the sympathy of others, our viewpoint is hardened into anger or a perpetual pity party. Some experts believe negative thinking is addictive. Fortunately, this destructive way of thinking can be broken by simply changing one's attitude. Changing peer groups around you can also be very healthy.

By determining to become happy, enthusiastic, and optimistic, we will soon become happy, enthusiastic, and optimistic. By thinking and speaking negatively we become negative. By thinking and speaking positively, we become positive. The choice is entirely up to each of us to determine what kind of person we wish to become, for ourselves and others.

Anxiety as an Ally

A major key to success is to develop and maintain

a success-oriented attitude from the very beginning. Overcoming self-doubt, anger, bitterness, and other self-defeating attitudes is often the greatest challenge. As John Belk of Belk Department Stores often advises, "Whining about your problems to others is a waste of time; half of them don't care and the other half are glad you've got them." This is an overstatement, of course, but the point is well made. Each of us must resolve to be either a winner or a whiner.

When trying to keep yourself on track to reaching your goals, you have reason to feel some anxiety. But you can leverage anxiety into a powerful ally for success. You see, a little anxiety keeps you mentally alert and drives you into action. Even if the worst happens and you get caught in a tailspin, do not panic. The good news is that we're in the middle of an expanding economy, and with the proper attitude, the odds of getting ahead are very good. Remember, you are simply a work in progress and so is everyone else!

"But life's been unfair to me," you may be thinking. Welcome to the club! Life is full of unfairness, unhappiness, and negativism. We can clamor all we want about the unfairness of life's circumstances, but absolutely nothing will change the circumstances unless we resolve to change them through conscious action. At this point in your life you may not feel in control. But you'll always have the option to be in control of one thing—your attitude. You see, it's not what happens *to* you that matters; it's what happens *in* you that matters. By controlling your attitude, in a certain sense, you control your destiny.

Working in an atmosphere of low morale is always difficult. Unfortunately, too many people choose to believe their morale is determined by their supervisors or by the actions of others. In truth, people should not allow their morale to be determined by anyone except themselves. Mature, successful people choose to be responsible for their morale, regardless of their circumstances.

Facing the Day

Only one person can decide how you will face each day. The temptation to seek safety, to avoid taking risks, to give up on dreams is forever around you. But positive people know how to keep faith in themselves and in their abilities. You can control your thoughts, and your thoughts control your emotions and attitudes. If you don't like the facts, you can change your attitude about them. It takes some practice, but millions of people do it every day. By looking at any situation from a detached viewpoint, you can begin to see different, even positive, dimensions of the situation. How many times have you worried yourself sick over something that never materialized? Or more likely, how many times have you experienced something terribly negative in your life only to see it as a positive growth experience in retrospect?

One technique that often helps to reduce excess anxiety or worry is to ask yourself the following questions when you are faced with a major problem:

☞   *Does it threaten my soul?*

☞   *Does it threaten my family?*

☞   *Does it threaten my life?*

☞   *How important will this be fifty or one hundred years from now?*

This exercise helps you get in control of your thoughts about any anxiety-producing condition by developing the proper perspective. Once you can control your thoughts, you can eliminate negative thinking and replace it with a positive, success-oriented attitude. You become a positive person simply by thinking positively!

Advice from the Pros

Successful people are noted for their persistent optimism and infectious cheerfulness. They are fun to be around because they are so encouraging.

In preparation for this book, I surveyed some of America's most prominent people and some not so well known. These successful people represent a variety of business types, sizes, and geographic locations and to verify what it takes to become influential. For this chapter, I surveyed two people, both of whom are extremely successful in their careers and learned how to become invaluable in their own right.

Zig Ziglar, a famous motivational speaker and writer, regularly participates in national speaking tours with notables like President George Bush and Barbara Bush, Colen Powell, Dr. Robert Schuller and others. He has written several best seller books focused on helping people achieve their dreams, and is chairman of the board of Ziglar Training Systems.

Zig has this to say about the importance of a good attitude: "Having a good attitude is extremely important for peak performance. With the right attitude you will acquire the other skills necessary for success."

Zig's advice to people who want to advance and become independent of circumstances is: "Develop and use the qualities of integrity, dependability, optimism, competence, enthusiasm, commitment, and hard work. Also, share your knowledge and enthusiasm to help others grow. Those who move ahead do so because they develop and teach others."

John Belk, Chairman of the Board for Belks, Inc. which operates over 250 department stores throughout the Southeast, also had a successful political career serving as the mayor of Charlotte, North Carolina. Business and political leaders from across the country seek Mr. Belk's expertise and advice.

John has this to say about the importance of a good attitude: "With a can do, optimistic attitude you can accomplish almost anything. With a [network of friends] who have this same positive attitude, [you] can accomplish almost anything and overcome nearly every adversity. Positive attitudes are essential for those who aspire to become influential."

Conclusion

People with successful lives almost always have a clear goal in mind, they have faith in themselves, and they jump into the self advancement process with relish. They make up their minds to view their goals as an adventure, and they see themselves as a desirable product or service to be marketed. Most of all, they have an unquenchable spirit of optimism and cheerfulness, and they know that the impressions they make on others are important, especially the first one. A constant review of the altitude of the attitude is essential for success. This law of attitude will contribute to your success and happiness more than any other law reviewed in this book.

Practical Advice

Remember, others value people who have good, "Can Do" attitudes. Make up your mind right now to concentrate on your blessings and your strengths, not your troubles. Make a conscious decision to be cheerful and optimistic. Demonstrate your positive attitude by practicing it in every situation and in everything you do. Try to focus all of your attention on the person or persons with whom you're talking. You especially need to be positive during all direct contacts with anyone who can potentially help you keep or advance toward your goals.

You must learn to control your attitude by thinking positively in all situations and at all times so that you, in fact, become positive. Your broad smile, confident posture, firm handshake, and sincere greeting are essential in making a good impression. I can tell you unequivocally that my impressions, good or bad, are always determined within the first minute or so of our meeting each other. Yes, sometimes that initial impression changes over time, but first impressions die hard, and most people never get a second chance to change that impression. Frankly, if there is no excitement in the eye, cheerfulness in the heart, and a genuine positive nature within a person they are in trouble. The lesson? Make that first impression a great one by having an uplifting, enthusiastic, and consistently positive attitude!

Points to Ponder

✧   Resolve to be happy.
✧   Stay positive.
✧   Success is attainable.
✧   Keep the faith.
✧   Make work an adventure.
✧   Impressions are lasting.

From This Day Forward

This section, which will appear at the end of each chapter, is designed to help you internalize and apply each law in your daily life.

- ◆ Example: "I will be cheerful, enthusiastic, and grateful for my blessings."

- ◆ Example: "I will not participate in whining, criticizing, or demeaning others."

- ◆ Example: "I will view my life as an adventure!"

- ◆ _____
  _____

- ◆ _____
  _____

- ◆ _____
  _____

Chapter Two

The Law of Communication

COMMUNICATE WELL OR FOREVER BE MISUNDERSTOOD

Many people think that technical skills and prior experience are the most important determinants for becoming influential in today's sophisticated society. They are wrong. Survey after survey of business leaders indicates that the most successful people are those who can communicate well. In fact, my research indicates that the possession of specific technical skills and prior experience rank low in achieving success in life. Of course, they play a role in success, but there are nine laws before them that are critical for becoming influential.

All the knowledge and technical skills known to humanity are useless unless you can communicate to other people. If you have good technical skills and experience in a given field, but you have problems getting, keeping, or advancing in relationships, the chances are high that you have violated the second law of becoming influential.

The Law of Communication underscores the critical dimension of communication. People judge us in large measure by the way we communicate. Unfair as it may sound, the truth is, people evaluate us by the way they see and hear us. Everyone communicates, but not everyone communicates effectively. The Law of Communicating to become influential emphasizes the need to (1) make a good impression, (2) project confidence, and (3) build trusting relationships quickly. People who become effective at using the law of communication in this respect will have few problems advancing in life and becoming influential to others.

You can demonstrate the truth of this law by answering the following questions:

☞ *How many really good communicators have I known who were out of work very long?*

☞ *If I had my choice to spend a social evening with a good communicator or a poor communicator, which one would I select?*

☞ *If an employer has the choice (and he or she usually has) of promoting a good com municator or a poor one, which applicant do I think will get the promotion?*

The ability to make effective group presentations is becoming increasingly important to personal success, but this law of communication mostly involves basic interpersonal communication skills. Leaders consistently rate verbal skills, nonverbal skills, and writing skills as key skills necessary for success. I have interviewed hundreds of people as potential associates who have had impeccable credentials, but their interviews, body language, and/or cover letters cost them any chance of serious consideration. With the knowledge base being equal, those with the best attitudes and best communication skills more easily reach their goals. One more thing, if you really want to achieve your goals, make sure you tell others about those goals. They will respect you for having set a clear vision and you will be on their mind when opportunities become available.

The Leader

Just put yourself in the shoes a leader you know for a moment. As the person making decisions about the organization, your credibility and judgment are on the line. Your success may well depend on your ability to identify the most productive people. If you are the owner of a company, your ability to search out the best people among many becomes even more essential. Further, your ability to build trusting relationships and mentor those you depend on becomes a critical skill. In fact, the very existence of your business may depend on your ability to influence others.

Advice from the Pros

Building trusting relationships is the secret of successful people the world over. This is especially true in business where communication, teamwork, and trust are so critical. Four nationally respected business leaders offer the following advice regarding the importance of interpersonal communication.

Rolfe Neill, former publisher of the Charlotte

Observer, an award winning Knight Ridder newspaper with a daily circulation of 240 thousand, views the ability to communicate as a critical human characteristic.

Rolfe had this to say about the importance of communication skills for peak performance: "Communications is the heart of all human relations, and human relations is at the heart of all human activity. Therefore, good communication skills are paramount-whether you're a janitor or a chairman."

Rolfe's advice to people who want to advance and become invaluable is: "Take any [task] given to you, do it better than anyone else, then ask for more."

Billy Ray, President of Bell South for North Carolina, and a renowned negotiator in federal telecommunications regulations, understands the importance of being able to communicate clearly.

Billy says this about the importance of communicating well: "Excellent communication skills are a must. These include: listening, leading by example, giving clear directions and expectations, inspiring confidence and motivating others. Good communication does not necessarily require a great vocabulary or excellent writing skills, but it does require the ability to connect with other people."

Billy's advice to people who want to advance and become invaluable is: "Be involved, be responsible, be a team player, and step forward to do the task with integrity and character."

William J. Ryan is Senior Vice President of Human Resources for Sea-Land Service, Incorporated, an international company that moves goods throughout the world in bulk containers on ships, railcars, airplanes, and trucks. This remarkable company operates in over 80 countries and employs approximately nine thousand people.

Bill says: "Effective communication is the cornerstone for effective leadership. It is the competency that is essential to be a leader."

Bill has this advice for people who wish to become influential: "Get involved and understand the global market and your business. Make things happen, take risks, and build friendships. . ."

Finally, Mark Ethridge, CEO for a multi-state publishing organization which produces weekly business journals has this input. "Having good communication skills is vital [for personal success]. It's not possible to be a peak performer without being a great communicator. What good is an idea if it can't be effectively shared?"

His advice to people who want to advance and become invaluable is straightforward: "Do more than is expected of you."

The secret to becoming influential, according to some of America's most respected people, is to learn to communicate well, be knowledgeable, and be more productive than everyone else.

Assess Yourself

You will do well to assess your communication strengths and weaknesses then conscientiously work to improve. Often, your best friend or your spouse will be honest enough to point them out to you. In any event, reading books, listening to tapes, and attending seminars on communication techniques is advisable. Brushing up on communication skills is always a good idea since these skills generally assist in all of life's endeavors. An assessment of your adeptness in the following areas will be most useful:

☞   Speech. Seek an honest critique of your ability to speak in casual and in formal settings. People especially value your skills at making presentations. Your peers value your interpersonal, conversational skills. Good telephone skills and etiquette are essential. Be sure your volume and intonation are adequate and your diction is good. Work at eliminating anything that distracts from your effectiveness when speaking.

☞   Body language. Believe it or not, your body language speaks volumes to the observer. Assess your posture in a variety of settings. Photographs and videotape recordings are especially revealing. Concentrate on holding eye contact, keeping pleasant facial expressions, and remaining poised in all circumstances.

29

☞ Writing. Get someone to review your writing skills, particularly as they apply to memorandums, reports, E-mail, and thank-you notes. Grammar checks and spell checks are nice on the computer, but they are no substitute for effective writing.

☞ Communication etiquette. Seek an honest assessment of your ability to listen well and to participate in social conversations. Do you encourage conversation by introducing topics and by asking questions of others? Do you stay focused on other people's thoughts or are your own more interesting to you?

☞ Paralanguage. The best conversationalist is an active listener. Does your paralanguage—verbal sounds of agreement, surprise, understanding, and disagreement, for example—encourage and compliment others when they're talking?

Many of these communication attributes come naturally to you. Others are not so natural, but you can learn them. However you choose to learn to communicate effectively, you must be able to gain people's confidence through sincerity. One technique for developing good communication skills is to emulate someone whom you think does well in this area. It could be a politician, a teacher, a salesperson, or anyone who has proven success in dealing with others on a consistent basis. Confidence comes from being prepared.

If you have a serious communication deficiency, do not lose heart. Helen Keller could neither speak, hear, nor talk yet she was graduated from Radcliffe and became an internationally famous author and lecturer. Consider Moses of Old Testament times. His brother Aaron often spoke for him in formal settings because Moses had a speech affliction. Yet Moses became one of the most important figures in his time or anyone else's.

Conclusion

Communicating effectively is an essential law for becoming influential. It begins with planning and ends with making a great impression on paper, electronically, and during day to day communication with others. Once you have chosen the path and goal you most wish to achieve, plan for it and develop the confidence that you will be the best among your peers.

Making a good impression seldom happens by accident. The secret to making a good impression is to become a good communicator. Listen to others as intently as you would listen to a toddler's first words. Be friendly, contribute to conversations, and always keep a sense of humor. Your subordinates, peers, and superiors will come to respect and appreciate you. We all value good communicators, people with vision, and people who are loyal to us and our business. Just be sincere and be yourself—your best self—and you will increase your chances of obtaining your goals. Strive to become a good communicator and you'll be astonished at how easy it is to make a good impression, project confidence, and build trusting relationships.

Practical Advice

Your attitude is extremely important, but your ability to communicate is also important. Make a conscious decision to assess your verbal and nonverbal communication skills, and resolve to improve by adopting techniques of successful people and by reading books, listening to tapes, and attending seminars. Answering anticipated questions with sincerity and thought is essential during all human interaction. But you must not overlook making a good impression through facial expressions, posture, and listening skills. The lesson? Be prepared, be sincere, and communicate with confidence!

Points to Ponder

✧ Learn to communicate well.
✧ Project confidence.
✧ Build trusting relationships.
✧ Make good impressions continuously.
✧ Evaluate strengths and weaknesses in communication.
✧ Read books, listen to tapes, and attend seminars

From This Day Forward

➥   I will communicate better by listening more and concentrating on the other person's problems and ideas.

➥   _____

_____

➥   _____

_____

➥   _____

_____

Chapter Three

The Law of Work Ethic

ANYTHING
WORTH DOING IS
WORTH DOING WELL

THE THIRD LAW FOR BECOMING INFLUENTIAL IS HAVING A STRONG WORK ETHIC.

"Just give me someone who is drug-free, on time, and has a good attitude - they'll have a successful career with us!" As I speak around the country about this subject, I hear the same exclamation. CEO's are desperate for workers with strong work ethic. Most of us value productive people with good work ethics. People who show up on time, are productive, and enjoy going that extra mile are inevitably more successful than those who show no enthusiasm or dedication.

Businesses are in the wealth creation business. They create products or provide services that generate a profit. This profit is inevitably spread into the economy as the company pays its employees, pays taxes, distributes bonuses to its marketing force, and spends money for expansion. People, lots of them, benefit from these wealth creating enterprises. In many respects, people and companies are pursuing the same goal – to better their condition through the acquisition of wealth. Smart people understand that loyalty and high productivity will help them better achieve their own goals for wealth and a better condition. Smart people value commitment and productivity. This, in its simplified form, is referred to as good work ethic. Free enterprise encourages a strong work ethic, and that is precisely what the market place rewards.

You can verify the truth of this important law by answering the following questions:

☞ *If I am paying someone to paint my house, do I want the painter to do a quick job, a mediocre job, or a thoroughly professional job including cleanup?*

☞ *If I'm paying someone by the hour to repair my automobile, how often would I want him to take breaks or chat with coworkers?*

☞ *When I've employed someone to repair my plumbing, do I expect it to be halfway, mostly, or totally fixed?*

Your answers are the same as everyone else's. We expect to get our money's worth from people we pay to render a service. After all, businesses are owned and operated by people just like the rest of us. American businessmen and businesswomen recognize that people make their business successful or unsuccessful, and that is why training and work ethic are so important to them. The only way businesses can survive in the global marketplace is to out produce or give better service than their competitors. And the only way they can out perform their competitors is through the use of excellent professionals who are willing to give 110 percent all the time. Loyalty is also an essential attribute of good work ethics.

The Profit Factor

In a free market economy, your ability to compete in the marketplace determines whether you make a profit or lose your shirt. You must understand these fundamental principles: *profit* is not a dirty word and financial security is directly tied to productivity. As cruel as it sounds, no one owes anyone else financial security. Further, no one should feel entitled to financial security unless their productivity and worth to the marketplace so justifies. Each of us earns our success by preparing for it and we keep it by helping the others reach their goals. In short, your ability to help others and out produce your competition ultimately determines your success.

In today's global economy, we can depend on one common truth: If a society wants to live well, it must produce well. I would take this truth one step farther and state if you want to live well, you must produce well. You see, people and their ability to out produce their competitors are the forces that really drive our economy. Government does not drive the economy, and neither does corporations; people drive it. Subsequently, individual productivity is directly related to individual economic success, just as the collective productivity of a business is directly related to it's economic success.

It is natural for us to want to make as much money as we can, to be appreciated for our work, and to be a part of something important. These things can be achieved through a strong work ethic. Successful businesses must have a collection of highly motivated, highly productive people. The attributes that can make you the best include sharing your success with others and rewarding productivity in others. Keep your commitments on time, give it your best every day, be honest and loyal, and go that extra mile - that is what having a strong work ethic is all about. Believe me, when work ethic and productivity are questioned, set backs occur. Today is your day, seize it and use it in your own special way!

What's the Motivation?

Motivation surveys consistently indicate that we are motivated by three primary factors:

◆ Recognition
◆ Being part of the team
◆ Fair compensation

An anonymous, but wise, author once said, "There's no traffic jam on the extra mile." Therein lies a golden opportunity for anyone seeking financial security. Knowing about the Law of Work Ethic, you can design your daily performance to emphasize your positive work habits. If you wonder how you are doing, just compare your work habits and productivity with your leaders.

Each day presents an opportunity to move past a former performance record and establish a better one. This attitude will cause you to resolve to give 110 percent right from the beginning and it will let others know they aren't your stepping stones. You are creating your own stepping stones and becoming the best. Others will be impressed with your drive and work ethic.

Advice From The Pros

Al Allison, III is the Executive Vice President of Allison Fence Company in Charlotte, North Carolina. His business is of small to medium size and is labor intensive. Al is on a constant crusade of encouraging educational institutions to turn out workers with better work ethics. His company, like thousands of others across America, is desperate for workers who will show up on time, work hard, and be dependable.

Al says this about the importance of a good work ethic for peak performing employees: "A strong work ethic is extremely important and may be the most important factor in valuing an employee's worth to the company!"

Al has this advice to people who would like to advance and become invaluable: "Build a strong work ethic in your character, take charge of your health both physically and spiritually, and become competent in the product or service you provide. Seek balance in your life and always give more than 100 percent—you will become invaluable!"

Richard Kipp is Vice President for Human Relations, Okuma America Corporation, a major prolucer of industrial lathe and milling machines, is an expert in customer relations, employee relations, and training collaboratives. He is a national speaker about the importance of workplace skills acquisition.

Rick says this about the importance of work ethic for those who wish to advance and be secure in their jobs: "A good work ethic is very important for all workers. Employees need to be empowered, work with minimal supervision, and complete tasks in a timely manner."

Rick has this advice to employees who would like to advance and become invaluable: "Become proficient in your current job. Become knowledgeable about the company and share your knowledge with others. Participate in cross-functional projects when ever possible. Be positive and demonstrate loyalty to the organization. Be a self-starter and complete all assignments. Continue your education, work on interpersonal skills, and be willing to do more than your job requires."

Valuable employees generally become indispensable because they are productive, dependable, loyal to the organization and their supervisors, and they always seek to do their best! Take it from the pros and follow their advice.

Conclusion

Just as you expect your automobile mechanic to fix your car promptly and reliably for a fair price, others expect you to do what you do with professionalism and competence. If you expect to be recognized for your efforts, appreciated, and compensated fairly, it's up to you to be the best. It's up to you to put out 110 percent each and every day.

To become influential, you must emphasize your commitment to your goals and underscore your strong work habits. Being honest, being a team player, sticking with it till the end, and being loyal to others are all critical traits influential people demonstrate.

Practical Advice

Projecting a positive attitude about life and about your goals is essential. Communicating enthusiasm for your goals is important, and having the work ethic to achieve those goals will help you become, and stay, successful. The secret to making a great impression is to be all that you say you are. Be enthusiastic and positive, communicate well, and be a professional who is willing to give 110 percent every day.

Finally, demonstrate your strengths when given the opportunity. Undoubtedly people will ask you to tell about yourself. This is your cue to talk about your goals and successes. Everyday chitchat about your roots, your family, and your training helps build good relationships, but remember to project your enthusiasm about your goals and the goals of others.

Points to Ponder

◇ Project enthusiasm.
◇ Project integrity.
◇ Project dependability.
◇ Project cooperation.
◇ Project competence.
◇ Project diligence.
◇ Project loyalty.
◇ Give 110 percent.

From This Day Forward

➡ I will work harder and smarter than I have before.

➡ I will give 110 percent to my daily goals.

➡ _____

_____

➡ _____

_____

➡ _____

_____

Chapter Four

The Law of Teamwork

IF YOU DON'T BELIEVE IN
COOPERATION, JUST
OBSERVE WHAT HAPPENS
TO A WAGON WHEN ONE
WHEEL COMES OFF.
—ANONYMOUS

> ## THE FOURTH LAW FOR
> ## BECOMING INFLUENTIAL IS
> ## BEING A TEAM PLAYER.

In much of our early childhood we are taught to be competitive, and we are rewarded for outperforming our peers. We quickly learn to compare our performance to the performance of others, and our self-images are developed in this way. It is no wonder that teamwork comes as a shock to many of us as we enter adulthood. With few exceptions achieving our goals requires good social skills and the ability to function as part of a team. Fortunately, most adults quickly develop a natural desire to be part of a team.

You can apply personal examples to verify the truth of the law of teamwork. Ask yourself the following questions:

☞ *Have I ever seen an effective organization that did not have a common purpose and good teamwork by its members?*

☞ *Is it possible for me to build a Delta II rocket by myself?*

☞ *How many loners have I really enjoyed working around?*

Many people miss out on the great things of life because of an inability to get along with others. We are

born to be gregarious, social beings. True joy comes from serving others, achieving goals, and being part of a team that is focused on worthy purposes.

The Need to Cooperate

If you seek advancement toward career goals, your reputation as a congenial team player will be an important asset. Your initial task is to remove all doubt about whether you are cooperative. If you have been uncooperative in the past, determine what you have learned from the experience, and then resolve to never repeat the mistake. Having a great attitude, communicating well, and displaying a good work ethic are critical, but if there is a lingering doubt about your ability to fit in and work well with others it may be your downfall. It is also important that you are viewed as a person who contributes to the goals or visions of others. Whether you are the janitor, in an accounting department, or own your own business, remember that your real business is the business of helping people and building relationships. Each contact with another person is an opportunity to build a positive life relationship. Everything you do should contribute to the common purpose of others. Working harmoniously with others is critical. Cooperation is essential not only for achieving a goal but also for keeping a happy, healthy, and productive life.

Balance Between Task and Team

If you are not sure about your ability to get along with others or whether you are perceived as a team player, reflect on your last or current job. Do people like you? Do your peers invite you to lunch? Do you share credit for tasks well done but accept responsibility for problems? Some people, particularly high achievers, are naturally more task oriented than team oriented. However, achieving a proper balance between being task and team oriented is a worthy goal.

I once worked with an absolutely brilliant man who could accomplish almost anything, as long as no one got in his way. People marveled at his passion for life and for his work. His peers appreciated his talent and admired his innovative ideas. His superiors—and I was one of them—loved his work as an individual, but were continually worried about whom he would offend next. Unfortunately, this talented individual could not work well with any ideas except his own. In consequence, he often felt it necessary to confront others about their "lousy" ideas and "stupid" opinions. Poor fellow, the last I knew he was jumping from job to job and being completely misunderstood and unappreciated.

The law of teamwork is fundamental to your success at becoming influential. Resolve now to talk less, listen more, criticize less, and praise more in every situation. You will feel better, and people will love you.

Consider the best conversationalists you have known. Without exception they will be people who listen well and with patience. When you were a youth, getting the credit for some outstanding feat or performance was integral for the development of a healthy self-image. Unfortunately, some people are so insecure that they continue to strive for all the praise and all the glory, even when the achievement could not have been accomplished without the assistance of others. It does not really matter who gets the glory as long as the work team is recognized. It's the old "you reap what you sow" principle at work here. As you praise others, praise will be returned. If you want to improve your situation, use this "listen more, praise more" attitude.

Being a team player also means contributing more than your fair share and being willing to try other people's ideas even when they make little sense. You can communicate this notion by demonstrating an ability to try out other's ideas and by getting along with others. In this respect, keeping a sense of humor is important. Recent research indicates that people who can laugh at themselves and with others are more creative, less rigid, and more willing to try new ideas.

Advice from the Pros

Jerry Richardson, founder and principal owner of the Carolina Panthers NFL team, understands full well the importance of teamwork. As a former NFL player and as a highly successful restaurant franchise owner, this remarkable man believes that teamwork is absolutely essential to career and business success.

Jerry gives this advice to people who want to be the best at what they do: "Treat everyone with respect and be trustworthy. Be competent and eager to learn. Work hard, be harmonious, be a team player, and listen well. Finally, be positive, do your best, and do what you say you will do."

Jim Morgan, CEO of Interstate Johnson Lane, a large brokerage firm located in Charlotte, North Carolina says: "Teamwork is critical at every level. We have learned over time that any one who tends to think in the first person singular will eventually hold back our performance and will fail individually."

Jim has this advice for people who hope to become influential: "I would advise them to never underestimate the importance of people skills. Obviously, intelligence and common sense are critical ingredients for success, but relationship skills are even more critical."

Conclusion

As social beings, the ability to build relationships is extremely important. If you hope to be successful, learn to become influential to others by serving them. Learn to listen, praise, and support other people's ideas. Team players are always valued for their ability to be friendly, helpful, and contented at all times. Personal success is unequivocally tied with service to others!

Practical Advice

Whether you are a good team player does not really matter if you are self-employed or financially independent. But if you are like the rest of us, you should be honing your social skills continuously. Learning to listen, praising others, and trying out the ideas of others are skills we can all learn and continue to improve. Try them at home with your family and with your friends. Before long, unless you are already expert at these skills, people will wonder what has come over you. Better yet, as you make a consistent effort to improve these skills, they will become second nature to you just when you need them most.

During a crucial part of the Second World War, General Dwight Eisenhower was told that his command desperately needed second lieutenants. There were no junior officers to be had, but General Eisenhower solved the problem quickly by ordering second lieutenant field commissions upon soldiers who were Eagle Scouts. The general was aware that the Scouts would know about leadership and teamwork, both basic characteristics for military officers. The general knew that the first part of the Boy Scout Law, for instance, required them to be "helpful, friendly, courteous, kind." People who wish to become influential will do well to follow the same code. Being helpful, friendly, courteous, and kind just about wraps it all up if you want to achieve your dreams.

Zig Ziglar, one of America's best motivational speakers and writers, reminds us that we can reach our successes if we help others reach theirs. We cannot expect to be successful alone. Come to think of it, even the Lone Ranger had Tonto to help!

Points to Ponder

✧ Build strong relationships.
✧ Learn to listen.
✧ Learn to praise.
✧ Try others' ideas.
✧ Illustrate success through teamwork.
✧ Be helpful, friendly, courteous, and kind.

From This Day Forward

●◆ I will concentrate on building strong, positive relationships.

●◆ _____
_____

●◆ _____
_____

●◆ _____
_____

Chapter Five

The Law of Problem Solving

IT IS BETTER TO
LIGHT A CANDLE THAN TO
CURSE THE DARKNESS.
—ANCIENT CHINESE
PROVERB

People are constantly on the lookout for others who can solve day-to-day problems. By adopting this law as a work habit, you will have no problems becoming influential. People enjoy associating with visionaries, but those who have the ability to solve problems are most valued by others.

You can easily verify the truth of the Law of Problem Solving by considering the following questions:

☞ *Which person would I rather have to take care of my lawn: one who cuts and trims only, or one who cuts, trims, feeds, seeds, and does whatever is necessary?*

☞ *Which automobile mechanic would I prefer: one who replaces parts according to symptoms, or one who searches out the cause before replacing parts?*

☞ *Who do I think would be most valued: one who says, "That's not my job," or one who says, "Let's see how we can fix this"?*

Obviously, we prefer being with and following people who have the confidence, ability, and personal incentive to solve problems. Anyone can dodge respon sibility by ignoring problems or by suggesting that problems are not their responsibility. However, those who want to do well in life will take on the challenges as they occur.

An Opportunity to Learn

As a college student, I worked full time at a television station as a technical engineer. I ran the cameras, audio board, film chain, videotape machines, and video switcher as assigned. I had to join a national labor organization to hold the position. One evening, while we were shooting a live commercial for an appliance store, a new television set began to slide off a shelf to the floor. A cameraman quickly steadied the television set whereupon a more seasoned employee chastised him. "That's not your job!" he bellowed. "Only the floor crew can touch things on the set. If you start doing things like that, they'll think they don't need a floor crew and we'll lose our jobs." You can buy into this attitude if you like, but it will be a violation of the problem solving law.

As a seasoned college president, I can spot problem solvers at my very first meeting with them. They have a special notion that they are part of the organization, and they delight in putting its goals above their own. They talk about solutions and opportunities to improve the college and its students rather than about problems or potential problems. They are optimistic, cheerful, cooperative, and customer focused.

A person who wishes to be significant to others will do well to remember that there are opportunities in every situation. Instead of whining or complaining about a situation, truly influential people seize the chance to solve problems and lead others by being positive. There really is a silver lining with every cloud.

Initiative, Imagination, and Ingenuity

Just how do you learn to practice the attributes of this law? First, you should clearly understand the organization's vision. What does the organization really want to become or accomplish? Once you understand the vision or primary goal, you should learn the parameters of your role in the business. Second, you should learn to exercise the three I's: Initiative, Imagination, and Ingenuity.

Take the initiative when problems emerge. It is okay if it does not work out right the first time or even the second or third time. The point is that you are willing to take the risk, to be the leader in a difficult situation. Remember, opportunity seldom comes to us on a platter; it's usually disguised as a major problem. Problem solvers also use their imagination. They enjoy thinking outside the norm. They solicit input from others and from as many sources as possible. They never lose the childhood excitement of discovery. There is no substitute for ingenuity. Being resourceful and clever about finding solutions to problems for the ingenious is a creative process. Each problem or difficulty can be approached as an opportunity to be innovative, an opportunity to assist the organization in reaching its vision.

Leadership

Leadership is a major part of the Law of Problem Solving. Leaders have the confidence to try new things, motivate people to work as a team, and accept the responsibility of failure. Leaders understand that failure is only an event. Someone once said that if at first you do not succeed, you are running about average. No one succeeds at everything. Sure, Ulysses S. Grant was a great general and went on to become the eighteenth president of our country, but before the Civil War he was unsuccessful in the military and in business. Yes, George Washington won the revolutionary war, but he lost the first eight of all nine battles of that war. As you resolve to become influential, try to demonstrate your leadership skills at every opportunity. Let the people you work with know that you are not afraid to take leadership roles in solving problems. Let them know you believe in sharing praise, but you can accept the blame alone if something goes wrong.

Famous Problem Solvers

President Franklin Delano Roosevelt exemplified the character of a problem solver. He served as president of the United States from 1933 until 1945. During that time, he led the nation through the worst depression and the most extensive foreign war in our country's history. His methods for stabilizing the country's economy and leading the war effort are still debated, but everyone concedes that he was a dynamic leader and an excellent problem solver. He faced formidable odds, including a physical disability, but he never ceased to use his resources to find solutions for the organization (country) he ran. He faced adversity with optimism and stress with unconcern.

Another famous problem solver received the Presidential Medal of Freedom in 1977, but he refused all cash awards for himself. Jonas Edward Salk created the polio vaccine at the University of Pittsburgh in 1953, and this terrible disease, which killed or disabled hundreds of thousands each year, has been virtually eradicated from the earth. Dr. Salk used all the resources and staff at hand to fix a problem for untold millions of people now and in the future.

Not all of us can become as famous as Roosevelt or Salk with the solutions we discover. But each one of us, solving one problem at a time, is contributing to the betterment of the organizations for which we work, the economy, and ourselves. Most important, by assuming the character of a problem solver, we increase our influence chances for success.

Advice from the Pros

Businesses the world over are interested in finding and keeping people who can think on their own and use initiative, imagination, and ingenuity at work. The following executives offer this advice to anyone who aspires to be the best.

Ron Harper, Chairman and Chief Executive Officer of Harper Companies International, and his wife Katherine, President of Harper Companies, own and operate one of America's most successful and respected Flexography manufacturing organizations. They produce highly sophisticated inking cylinder equipment for the Flexography printing industry.

Ron has this to say about the importance of the ability and interest in solving problems in business: "It is extremely important for peak performers to be able to solve problems. The best [performers] accept accountability, take risks, and take charge of problems. They generally consider their options and solicit opinions from others before moving forward."

Ron gives this advice to people who would like to be considered influential: "Read! Study successful people and nurture a positive attitude. Take calculated risks, get involved, and go the extra mile every day."

Tom Moser, National Director for Consumer Markets for KPMG Peat Marwick, a nationally respected accounting firm, says this about the importance of having good problem solving abilities: "It is very important to learn how to access relevant information quickly and to learn how to involve others in arriving at the best decisions."

Tom has this advice for people who wish to excel at their goals: "Learn how to work well in teams and complex organizations."

Conclusion

People want to work with problem solvers. They are eager to associate with people who will take the initiative to improve. Wise people acknowledge the importance of the Law of Problem Solving and seize opportunities to demonstrate initiative, imagination, and ingenuity. Successful people exhibit leadership skills by demonstrating belief in themselves and in the value of teamwork. Above all, successful problem solvers continually ask themselves how they can help others improve their lives.

Practical Advice

Demonstrate your willingness to seize opportunities to solve problems at home, in social settings, and in business. Always be quick to offer solutions to problems. Anyone can articulate problems, but few people provide solutions to them. Solve problems and you will become influential to others.

Points to Ponder

✧ See problems as opportunities.
✧ Project initiative.
✧ Project imagination.
✧ Project ingenuity.
✧ Be a leader.
✧ Believe in yourself (and others).

From This Day Forward

⊷ I will trust my instincts and attempt to solve problems as they occur.

⊷ _____
_____

⊷ _____
_____

⊷ _____
_____

Chapter Six

The Law of Results

OUR GRAND BUSINESS IS
NOT TO SEE WHAT LIES
DIMLY AT A DISTANCE,
BUT TO DO WHAT LIES
CLEARLY AT HAND.
—THOMAS CARLYLE

The Sixth Law for Becoming Influential is To be Result Oriented!

Successful people become influential because they gain the ability to make a difference for others. They become successful because they are committed to helping others succeed. The whole notion of becoming significant is always accomplished in a social context. Zig Ziglar became a national phenomenon with his first book, See You at the Top! He became a national treasure years later when he wrote his book, Over the Top, which focused on moving from personal success to significance for others. Helping others solve problems and achieve results is the key to becoming truly significant and influential in the lives of others.

You can verify the truth of this successful career trait by asking yourself the following questions:

☞ *When my child or I last needed medical care, was I more concerned with completing the health insurance verifications or with seeing the doctor?*

☞ *Have I ever been given the run-around by a company when I needed repairs on something still under warranty?*

☞ *Did I ever need to pick up the laundry, but the cleaners didn't have it ready?*

Most of us have experienced the frustration associated with one or all three of the above illustrations. As consumers, we are interested in immediate attention, no lectures, and no run-around. Is it any wonder that we value action-oriented, results-seeking people?

If you have ever had to wait for an auto part or for a certain fabric to be available, you can understand why you need to complete your projects on time. If people cannot get what they want in a timely manner, they will take their business elsewhere. You should understand this basic relationship between people, and learn to focus on helping others solve their problems.

Getting Things Done

A cheerful, engaging attitude is nice, but it is not enough to become truly influential. To become invaluable, you have to convince others that you can get things done and that you will help them make more money. In short, you are an enterprise that will accomplish tasks for others in a results-focused manner. Influential people understand how to work within acceptable parameters and procedures and get things done in an exemplary fashion.

How busy you are and how busy you look have little to do with actual productivity or accomplishment. A person can be busy all day and all week, but never come to closure on anything of value to others or to a business. Work has a way of expanding to fill the time allot ted for it. A number of productivity studies have proved this principle. Motivated people consciously focus on getting things done to the very best of their ability in a timely manner. These people seem to have an intuition for being productive and they are highly appreciated by everyone.

We've all witnessed people whose desks are overflowing with papers. Usually, their office chairs and tables are also loaded with paperwork. They think this office demeanor projects how important they are and how hard they work. In reality, their office condition projects disorganization, confusion, and insecurity. Either they are thoroughly disorganized and inherently messy, or they are attempting to boast about how much work they do. In either case, such a display indicates that these people are process-oriented as opposed to results-oriented. Results-oriented people are eager to get things done and move the paperwork along. Results-oriented people have a strong need to reach the goal and move to the next challenge. Their desks are generally kept clean and uncluttered to be prepared for the next goal.

Character Flaws

Some people are simply lazy. For some inexplicable reason these folks would rather put off the goal than jump into it. They are almost never productive. Even if they manage to set a goal, their chances of reaching it are slim. Such behavior is wasteful for themselves and their business. Believe me, most people can spot someone who is lazy faster than a speeding bullet.

I have known many lazy people in my career. Unfortunately, the worst ones are almost always very intelligent. Such people work harder to keep from working than doing their assignments in the first place. I have yet to find a good explanation for such behavior, but I have learned to identify these people with great accuracy. Most of them would be excellent if they could eliminate that one character flaw. The point? Businesses and organizations exist by providing products or services. Everyone must carry his or her share of the load. If you hope to keep a cushy job where you do little work, you may as well throw in the towel now. You will be found out. Ignoring this law of action and results is one of the surest ways of becoming dispensable. As you seek to become invaluable, project the image of a results-oriented, hardworking, enthusiastic person who looks for solutions, not excuses.

Everyone can find excuses for not getting things done. Some people become experts at the art of excuses. They generally blame others, blame the product, blame the customers, blame the company, or blame some condition beyond their control for poor performance. In truth, we generally have no one to blame but ourselves for poor performance. Do not listen to others who help you find excuses or tell you some task cannot be done or is unreasonable. Above all, do not listen to yourself when you begin to think negatively. Successful professionals learn to focus on completing tasks, no matter how difficult, with a positive mental attitude. When you work, avoid espousing excuses just as you avoid using profanity. Your reputation must be impeccable. You never know who talks to whom about you.

Change Is A Part of Life

If you have become process-focused try to shift that focus toward solutions and results. Not so long ago people were outraged to hear that a long distance bus driver made an eighty-nine year old woman get off his bus on a lonely highway at night when he discovered she had a small dog. Company policy was being violated and this process-oriented champion did his duty. By using such poor judgment, however, the bus driver created a public relations nightmare for his company.

As president of a college, I often go to where our customers are being served to get an eyewitness account of our services. On one such occasion, at the beginning of a new semester, I saw two very long lines in the bookstore. Some lines are to be expected during this time since all students are buying new books and supplies for their classes. To my amazement, the students were standing for twenty or thirty minutes in the first line to present their book list and receive their books from a clerk. The students then stood in another line for twenty or thirty minutes to pay for the books! I asked for an explanation from the bookstore manager, but I was less than satisfied. After making a few suggestions and hoping that some creativity would emerge from the manager, her response was, "But that's how we always do it." You can imagine how much confidence I gained in that person at that moment.

You can stay results oriented if you constantly remind yourself of your primary goal. When the process interferes with your primary goal, you have an obligation to change the process within your control or request a change in the processes outside your control.

In all problematic situations you should ask yourself two basic questions: (1) Is it good for customers? and (2) Is it good for business? If the answers are in the positive and your solution is legal, you will seldom be wrong, even if a particular procedure or process says otherwise.

Becoming process oriented is generally nonproductive and unbelievably bureaucratic. Take a look at the Internal Revenue Service if you want to experience process orientation at its worst. The IRS code alone has more than seven million words, most of which are left to interpretation! Becoming process oriented is a trap that all professionals should avoid.

Advice from the Pros

Being results oriented and prone to action is a common characteristic among successful people. It is natural to value these same characteristics in other people. John Correnti, Former President and CEO of Nucor Corporation, the nation's second largest producer of steel products, exemplifies this law.

When asked how important results orientation is for peak performing people, he had this to say: "Being results oriented is very important. . . Always give more than is expected. Never, never give up on any assignment or duty. Be a good listener and learn how to communicate on every level, lowest to highest."

Kris Friedrich, founder and CEO of Money Mailer, the largest mail-based advertiser in the country, is keenly interested in associating with high performance people. He has this to say: "It is extremely important to be results-oriented and it is the key to balanced success. Don't just be focused on your own goals but be focused on other's goals as well. Do not be self-limited. Have specific performance standards and stick to them."

Kris's advice to people who desire to be the best is this: "Begin with a dream then set goals. Take action and set realistic time frames in which to reach your goals. Be visible! Take risks! Step up to the plate and out of the box!

Conclusion

People are valued for their ability to get things accomplished. People want to be associated with those who understand the importance of being results oriented, with people who have a natural desire to be productive and focus on the goal. Influential people will put this law of action into practice day after day. A distinct asset of a professional is a solid reputation for getting things done.

Practical Advice

Projecting a work ethic that includes a bias for action and an interest in achieving results will pay big dividends. Successful people always avoid any behavior that could damage their reputation. Laziness, negative thinking, and a bureaucratic mentality should be avoided at all costs. Remember, we value people who have a strong need for closure and who enjoy getting things done in a timely and professional manner. We enjoy being around results oriented people.

Points to Ponder

✧ Have a bias for action.
✧ Focus on results.
✧ Have a strong need for closure.
✧ Build a good reputation.

From This Day Forward

● I will work for results and attempt to change processes that interfere with results.

● _____
_____

● _____
_____

Chapter Seven

The Law of Organization

ORDER IS LIGHT,
PEACE, INNER FREEDOM,
SELF-DETERMINATION:
IT IS POWER.
—HENRI FREDERIC AMIEL

Accomplishing your work in an effective manner is the essence of the Law of Organization. One secret for always being effective and reaching your goals is to be organized. If you have no goal or specific objective, you will likely be unhappy with what you are doing. If you have a personal objective but do not develop or work a plan to achieve it, you will fail. No one can reach a goal unless it has been clearly identified and it is accompanied with a plan for its accomplishment. In short, if you want a dream to come true, get your act together.

You can easily validate the truth of this law by considering the following questions:

☞ *If I wanted to drive from Atlanta to Denver, would I consult a map?*

☞ *Would I rather have a well organized or a disorganized teacher for my six-year-old?*

☞ *Do I prefer to fly with pilots who file flight plans?*

Most people spend more time planning for a family reunion or a Fourth of July picnic than for their goals. Just a little planning can help you take advantage of the Law of Organization. Planning and diligent effort are the keystones to personal and financial success.

Staying Organized

Have you ever felt like you were spinning your wheels and not really accomplishing very much? If you haven't felt like this, you are truly unusual. Everyone has days where things just don't quite fit together; the computer breaks down, the right people are not available, or the information to move forward is unavailable. In spite of these inevitable frustrations, influential people always seem to find a way to get the job done. How do they do it? By being organized and staying focused on the important goals to be completed.

The following is a simple formula for being organized and effective in business or at the workplace:

◆ Understand the Mission or Vision
◆ Prioritize goals
◆ One thing at a time
◆ Evaluate for improvement

I once knew someone who spent more time writing a monthly newsletter than leading his business in accomplishing its essential goals. He failed to concentrate on the important aspects and was out of the business within a year. Common sense in prioritizing your daily goals and emphasizing essential goals will help you rise above the crowd.

Thinking in a logical manner is also a valuable attribute. A checker player who seldom thinks beyond one or two moves doesn't win many games. A person who does business in the same way is seldom very productive.

Once the mission or vision has been established and a sequence of goals has been mentally reviewed, it is important to stay focused on one goal at a time. If we constantly remind ourselves of how big or impossible a mission is, we will ultimately become discouraged and fail. Good time managers understand that you can only eat an elephant one bite at a time. Therefore, stick to each goal until it is finished, before worrying too much about the next one.

Finally, influential people understand that when it comes to quality and time, there is no finish line. These valued people regularly evaluate their goals in order to improve upon them. They continuously evaluate their goals informally by thinking about ways to improve. They often evaluate their performance in a more formal manner by seeking input from others. Successful people continuously measure their ability to influence other in a social context and they understand the importance of building and maintaining trusting relationships.

Advice from the Pros

Being well organized is prized and respected by everyone. Charles Davidson, President and Chief Executive Officer of J. A. Jones Construction, a multi-billion dollar, international construction corporation, has this to say about the importance of being organized:

"It is extremely important to be organized [in business]. Eighty percent of what we do is the necessary work that maintains the momentum of our business. Being organized allows us to perform this necessary work efficiently."

Charlie has this advice for people who would like to advance and become invaluable: "Lead a balanced life. Commit significant portions of each day to the development of your spiritual, intellectual, physical, and social well being. An absence of growth in any one of these four lifelong functions can adversely affect the other three."

Katie Tyler, a recent businesswoman of the year in Charlotte, North Carolina owns and operates a successful mid-sized construction company. She responded that, "Being organized isn't important, it is essential!" She offers this advice to people who wish to advance and become invaluable: "Write an essay of how your life will be when you become who you want to be. Include a reference to your [business] and how you will interact with it. Also describe your family life and personal life, then share this essay with everyone involved . . . This will help to make your life's plan into reality."

Tony Fortino, a highly successful automobile dealer, real estate entrepreneur, and small businessman in Pueblo, Colorado agrees that being organized is very important. His advice to people who want to excel in business is: Do your job with enthusiasm and a positive attitude. Always learn as much as possible about your [business]."

What Is Your Business Potential?

Choosing the perfect business can be frustrating and confusing. After all, your long-term success and satisfaction depends upon this critical selection. Fortunately, most people eventually gravitate toward a business they enjoy. Many others, however, drift from business to business and never find one that is truly rewarding.

You can take the guesswork out of the business selection process by understanding your interests, values, and abilities. As you compare probable businesses to your interests, values, and abilities, the identification of a business category eventually becomes evident. Consider exceptional athletes or scholars. They first discover their unique interests and abilities, then they select the sport or academic area they most value. By capitalizing on their basic interests, abilities, and values, they practice to become exceptional. The same principle holds true for people who successfully match their special interests and skills to a business that allows them to flourish.

Further, you should choose a business that you really value. Frankly, it does not matter what others think you can do. What matters is what you think and what you truly wish to do with your life. I am in my fifteenth year as a college president, I have a doctorate, have written twelve books, and I have achieved national acclaim in some educational circles. Yet two high school teachers told me that I was "not college material." You can be anything you wish to be if you want it badly enough and are willing to do what it takes. The desire to achieve a goal is fundamental to personal success.

Most people believe that IQ, grades in high school, and socioeconomic condition are the primary predictors of their future success. They are wrong. The most accurate predictors of future success include a moral character and a vision with the desire and self-discipline to pursue that vision. Your personal motivation to reach a goal or to succeed at a vision will determine your success. Your consistent zeal for and focus on the goal are paramount if you hope to achieve your personal vision. For this reason, select a career vision that you truly value and fully expect you can accomplish. If you neither value nor expect to reach the vision, you will fail.

In the early seventies, I taught two young college broadcasting students whose academic conditions were dissimilar. John's performance in the classroom was below average. Gary's academic record was exemplary. John's grades dropped so that a colleague counseled with him. "It is obvious you are not very interested in your studies, John. Just what is it you would really like to do?" my fellow teacher asked. "I'd really like to make music," John replied. We suggested that he should try it. A few years later John Cougar Mellencamp hit the charts as one of America's top rock and roll stars!

From my first meeting with Gary, he told me he was going to be the voice of the Indianapolis 500 and would be a television network announcer for auto racing. His grades were always outstanding, and he was graduated with a degree in broadcasting without a slip. A few years later, Gary Lee was recognized throughout the country as the ESPN anchor for auto racing.

What attributes propelled both young men into their nationally recognized careers? It was not their academic success or their economic status. The vision and persistence in achieving it were the attributes that made them so successful. They both set a goal that they highly valued and expected they could reach. They focused on that which they desired to become.

Of course, you must see yourself clearly and objectively. It is unrealistic to think you can become a professional baseball player just because you want to be famous and make a big salary. Even Michael Jordan, one of the greatest NBA players of all time, tried to make it in professional baseball but failed to excel in that sport. It is equally unrealistic to think you should become an astronaut unless you're willing to get the education and training required for that competitive career. If you exaggerate or minimize your interests or abilities, the result will likely be unpleasant. Be true to yourself when you select your next life goal or long-term vision.

Take note: Before you can accomplish anything, you must truly want whatever is to be accomplished. Motivation is linked directly to what you value plus your belief that you can attain it.

Developing a Plan of Action

People never accomplish much without thinking about what they want and how to best go about getting it. Since achieving your goal takes effort, it is prudent to develop a plan and follow it. This plan should be action oriented. Achieving your goal should require you to take a series of actions, from determining your daily effort to determining the most effective path to personal success. The following components are recommended for an effective action plan:

◆ Research needed skills
◆ Determine the best path to success
◆ Develop a list of people who can help
◆ Develop a plan for networking
◆ Develop a follow through system

The first step in developing a plan toward achieving your goal is to determine what skills are necessary. I recommend that you talk to your peers, someone who has attained the success you aspire to reach.

Determining the best path to achieve your goal is to first, resolve to become a person who is influential to others. Then talk with people in your chosen business to identify the most common path successful people have followed in that particular business. In the broadcasting industry, experienced sales people, rather than engineers or program people, usually become general managers. College presidents have most frequently come from instructional ranks, rather than from finance or student services. Successful entrepreneurs are almost always socially adept and focused.

Making a list of people to talk with can be a valuable exercise, but only if you talk with them. Most people love to talk about themselves and enjoy being asked for advice about their business field. Be bold and visit with people who can give you good advice.

Networking is extremely beneficial and a simple follow-up habit of sending thank you notes is always wise.

Networking Effectively

Once you have a clear career vision and a plan for achieving it, you will increase your chances for success by learning to network with anyone and everyone who can help in your pursuits. Networking is a business boosting skill that you can learn to do well. The secret is to become good at making friends. The purpose of networking is to help you generate new contacts. In effect, each person you talk to about your career has the potential to become a career consultant to you at no cost. Networking can be fun, exhilarating, and effective if you are prepared. The best people to help you achieve your vision are usually the people you associate with every day. Your peers can become the foundation for your success. Business hoppers often think they are climbing the ladder. Unfortunately, they fail to build a base of support and they end up building their business on a house of cards. As friends and associates help you climb your ladder to success, remember them and stay in contact as much as possible. In the end it is your business reputation and personal relationships that will make you successful. One last suggestion, as you get the opportunity to help others achieve their dreams, consider it as a privilege, not an obligation.

To be an effective networker, you should take every opportunity to be with people and to win friends who can help you. Becoming a good communicator is relatively easy if you follow this formula for successful communication: listen, listen, and listen some more. Most of us have two ears and only one mouth. God had good reasons for this configuration. Invariably, study after study on communication indicates that the best communicators are those who have the patience and wisdom to listen. That means listening before responding, avoiding interrupting the speaker, and listening some more. This one communication skill can do wonders for your relationships. You should also ask how you might be able to help those with whom you are networking. Building relationships is the key.

Occasionally, you will meet with people who do not speak freely. You need to find out about their interests as quickly as possible and focus on these things. If you are meeting someone, do some preliminary homework. Get a biographical description from someone who knows him. In this way you can get a feeling for his interests, and you can discuss your commonalties. The closer someone can connect with you, the more likely he will support you.

While in conversation with leaders in your business, do not miss the chance to ask for advice about your goal. Asking for advice is a sign of self-confidence, a sign of respect for the other person, and it is flattering. Once they give you advice, you must make every effort to use it and tell them how it helped. This situation will reinforce your relationship, and they will develop a greater commitment toward your success. It should go without saying that you should send a handwritten thank-you note to everyone who helps you even a little bit.

Finally, you should make a conscious effort to become as literate as possible with the issues surrounding your targeted objective. You will become infinitely more believable as you become conversant about your business. Read everything you can find about your business, talk, listen, and listen some more to people in that same business.

Conclusion

People want to be associated with self-motivated individuals who know what they want and are well organized. Successful people embody these characteristics to reach their goals. Envisioning a long-term business and staying focused on immediate short term goals are the first steps toward achieving the Law of Organization. Learning to plan and network effectively are two additional important steps toward becoming successful in your business. Being well organized projects confidence, reliability, and an impressive reputation to others. You can display all the behaviors represented by the other eight laws and still be unsuccessful if you are disorganized. Ignoring this law will be disastrous.

Practical Advice

Getting organized—and staying that way—is the surest method for becoming influential.

Points to Ponder

✧ Organize each business day
✧ Set a vision
✧ Develop an action plan
✧ Follow the action plan
✧ Learn to network

From This Day Forward

✒ I will plan my business strategy based on my ultimate goal.

✒ _____
_____

✒ _____
_____

Chapter Eight

The Law of Self-Confidence

EARLY IMPRESSIONS ARE
HARD TO ERADICATE
FROM THE MIND.
—JEROME

THE EIGTH LAW FOR BECOMING INFLUENTIAL IS BEING SELF-CONFIDENT!

Once you have determined your business or career vision and have developed a plan for getting it, you must focus your attention on the job of selling yourself. You must learn to put yourself in the place of those who can help you. They will be looking for evidence of the Nine Essential Laws for Becoming Influential as described in this book. They will be looking for someone in whom they can have confidence, someone in whom their expectations can be met. They will be looking for someone who has confidence in themselves.

You can verify the truth of this law by asking yourself the following questions:

☞   *When I last bought an automobile, was the credibility of the salesperson important to me?*

☞   *When I last chose a bank, a physician, or a veterinarian, did the reputation affect my choice?*

☞   *When I visited my child's school, how long did it take to get an impression of his or her teachers?*

Certainly, a person's credibility, reputation, and impression are important to us when we consider purchasing goods or services from them. The same principle is true of people in general. Self-esteem exhibits itself in many ways, and a healthy sense of confidence is important. But the impression you make on others is critical when you seek to become appreciated.

As you network, consider everyone you come into contact with as potentially helpful in the achievement of your career vision. Always put your best foot forward. This is a small world, and your reputation depends on what other people think of you. Each person you meet, especially in business, presents an opportunity for you to build a stronger and stronger reputation. Your reputation is your most powerful asset for becoming influential to others.

The First Sixty Seconds

The first sixty seconds of an encounter with a stranger are most lasting! There is much truth in the adage that we never get a second chance to make a first impression. Human beings are social beings. We exist in a world where our social experiences, that is our relationships with others, form the essence of our lives. All of us have learned to develop instant opinions of other people based upon the way we perceive them through their reputations and personal demeanor.

Your objective is to sell your worth to others on a daily basis, not by taking credit for every good accomplishment, but by giving your best every day. In a real sense, you should view yourself as an individual enterprise. In this way, your skills and talents will translate into value for yourself and others. The critical first sixty seconds of each social contact is your most important asset for advancements - if you know how to put your best foot forward and project confidence.

Be Mentally Prepared

First things first. Many coaches are fond of saying to their athletes, "Get your head on straight." The same advice holds true for becoming influential. You must project confidence, enthusiasm, and trustworthiness. Your comfort level in difficult situations will increase in direct proportion to your preparation for these events. To this end you should spend some serious time talking about your life vision and how you plan to achieve it.

Your vision is a clear picture of where you would like to be and what you would like to be doing with your life five, ten, and even twenty years from now. Your ability to clearly explain your vision to others will affect your chances for achieving that vision. You need to know where you want to go and how your career interests can help others meet their needs. For example, visions are self-centered, but the way you relate yours to others should be centered on how you intend to help others. People want to know what you can do for them, not what they can do for you.

Once an applicant spent five minutes in an interview telling me why the job she had applied for would be so important for her career aspirations. She never understood that I was more interested in what she could do for our organization than what we could do to further her career. Some people believe they are entitled to a job or a promotion. But believe me, an entitlement attitude will guarantee failure.

Essentially, your vision should describe what you are seeking and the contributions you hope to make to others in reaching it.

Be Spiritually Prepared

Being prepared mentally is essential, but it is often not enough. Influential people are usually at peace with themselves, and they have enough faith in God and in themselves to sustain them during any situation. Further, they accept rejections professionally with the understanding that rejections should not be taken personally. Finally, they have the heartfelt assurance that another opportunity to further their cause will soon evolve and that in the long run, all things happen for their good.

You can boost your spiritual preparation by associating with other persons of your faith. Two of the best methods for increasing spirituality are by encouraging others and through personal prayer. Most people easily recognize the self-confidence that usually results from a solid spiritual foundation. People who are spiritually as well as mentally prepared have confidence and naturally put their best foot forward!

Be Physically Prepared

Becoming influential will require all the physical stamina you can muster. Each situation has its share of stress and sometimes strenuous activity. Getting and staying in the best physical shape possible will heighten your chances for success. If you are not now in proper physical condition, there may never be a better time to exercise and eat a proper diet.

Your appearance can be your best asset or your worst liability when you interact with people. Your first and continuous impression will make a dramatic impact on them. The time to assess your overall visual and vocal impression is now—not a day or two before a business enhancing opportunity occurs.

It is sad but true; people treat you as they perceive you. Your first visual and verbal association with others will set off a whole series of judgments about your character and abilities. Even your handshake will project volumes about you. "But that's not fair," you may retort. Perhaps it is not fair, but people the world over process information and draw conclusions from that information the same way that you evaluate car salespeople, physicians, or teachers.

Your dress, hygiene, breath, posture, grooming, body language, facial expressions, and speech contribute to your ability to make good impressions. You should display an attitude of alertness, vitality, and confidence under all situations associated with your business. That also includes informal times when people observe you without your knowledge.

You are well advised to develop your appearance according to that expected of people in the level of leadership you most desire. Successful professionals pay close attention to their appearance. Their clothing, hair presentation, and accessories are consistently appropriate for their business. Basically, they present a conservative appearance that does not detract from the information exchange process. Successful people also employ good posture, make frequent eye contact, and smile easily. Of course, they also converse easily and succinctly. Anyone who aspires to become successful should be his or her best at dressing, posture, grooming, and articulating at all times.

Your speech should be natural with appropriate volume and clear diction. Having to exert a special effort to hear or understand you will make a negative impression on people. Certainly, eye contact and moderate smiling are essential elements for making good impressions. Don't play any power games by demonstrating your assertiveness or your ability to dominate. Be yourself, be courteous, be professional, and be in the best physical shape possible. Remember that you will be making impressions with everyone you meet, and you never know who or what group of people can help you reach your life vision or goal to become influential.

Be Socially Prepared

Your whole attitude should be to make as many friends as possible. People help people, and they usually help ones they know and like. The more friends you have, the better your chances for influencing others and achieving personal success. Smiles, good listening skills, and thank-you notes become valuable tools in the socializing process.

One other thing to consider: business is competitive by nature. As you attempt to project yourself as the most productive, friendly person in your field, ask yourself this question: *"If I were to compete with myself, what would I do?"* The answer to this question will help you become very competitive indeed!.

Advice from the Pros

Presenting a strong professional image is a hallmark of successful people. Dale Halton, President and CEO of a large Pepsi Cola Bottling franchise in Charlotte, North Carolina epitomizes this characteristic and expects the same from her people and suppliers. She says that "A professional image is very important for [people] who wish to advance. They set the tone for all those [on their team] and need to represent [themselves] in a professional manner at all times." Her advice to people who would like to become invaluable is: "Work hard and be honest. Represent [yourself] in a professional manner at all times and be open to seeking new opportunities and challenges."

J. Frank Harrison III is the president and CEO of a Coca Cola Bottling franchise headquartered in Charlotte, North Carolina. He says professional image is very important because "Right or wrong, people are initially judged by how they dress, their demeanor, etc." His advice to people who want to succeed is as follows: "Continuously work on the following areas:

- ◆ Your character
- ◆ Your skills
- ◆ Your trustworthiness
- ◆ Your listening ability
- ◆ Your ability to communicate at all levels."

Conclusion

Projecting healthy self-confidence is a sure way to achieving success. People want to associate with people they feel good about, people they like. Your ability to make a great impression before, during, and after a social or business situation will determine whether you succeed. The first sixty seconds of any new personal contact are critical. Everything about you, especially your attitude, communication skills, and personal demeanor, plays a part in how the others perceive you. Be mentally, spiritually, physically, and socially prepared. Anticipating questions and having honest, believable answers will carry you to success.

Practical Advice

Projecting a positive, friendly attitude with a professional demeanor is a foolproof formula for personal and business success. People help others who are productive and likable. Successful people know how to be on their best behavior at all times and they think of themselves as enterprises. Influential people do not feel entitled to business success, but they are willing to earn it by being their best before, during, and after every networking situation.

Points to Ponder

✧   Learn to sell yourself.
✧   Know what you want.
✧   Be mentally, spiritually, physically, and socially prepared.
✧   Recognize that the first sixty seconds are most important.

From This Day Forward

➽   I will be my best in all social and business situations.

➽   _____

_____

Chapter Nine

The Law of Learning

THE EDUCATION OF A MAN

IS NEVER COMPLETED

UNTIL HE DIES.

—ROBERT E. LEE

THE NINTH LAW FOR BECOMING INFLUENTIAL IS BEING AN ACTIVE LEARNER!

People who cannot or will not continue learning will not reach the personal or business success they hope to achieve. People who are not active in learning new skills and new behaviors are viewed as dull and uninteresting.

You can verify this law by asking yourself the following questions:

☞ *If I owned a secretarial service and one employee refused or could not learn to operate the new, more efficient word processing software, would I (a) allow her to keep using the old software or (b) replace her with an employee who could operate the new software?*

☞ *I am interviewing equally qualified applicants, but one shows evidence of active learning throughout the career. Which applicant would have the edge?*

☞ *Which type of person is most valued by leadership: a passive, methodical person or an active person who is eager to learn new skills and techniques?*

The correct answers are obvious, but they illustrate the point. The American marketplace is changing rapidly, and the academic, technical, and behavioral skills required for people in all fields demand continuous learning. Your willingness to gain new skills to be more productive represents the active learner law. Sometimes the learning curve, or demand for new skills acquisition, is steep (fast), and sometimes it is rather flat (slow). In either case, we are in a new environment that requires increased learning and new skills throughout our lifetimes.

As a young boy in the 1950s, I was curious why our neighbor, a grizzled and reclusive older man we called Fuzzy, seemed to be so poor, yet never worked to earn any money. Our family of ten always had plenty to eat, but everyone worked. "Fuzzy has a rough way of it, son," my father explained. "You see, he used to be a well digger, but modern technology came along, and he didn't keep up with it, so he was pushed out of a job." That incident made a lasting impression on me. If anything, the changing technologies at the workplace today are occurring at lightning speed compared to the changes in the early fifties. We no longer live in a predictable world where we can expect to earn a living by the sweat of our brow. We no longer live in a world where we can expect to work for the same company in the same basic position until retirement. Just as poor Fuzzy pushed himself out of a job for not learning new skills, today's workers are suffering the same fate with greater frequency. The tragedy is that it is not necessary to be unsuccessful because of a skills deficiency.

The opportunity to learn new academic, technical, or social- behavioral skills has never been better. Most leaders recognize the importance of keeping a well-trained organization and encourage or even provide training for their people. In short, if you need to acquire new skills, there is little excuse for not doing so.

If you wish to be among the most sought-after people for a position of leadership, learn the behavioral and leadership skills sought by your leaders, and make sure your leaders know what you have learned from them.

As you pursue your long-term goal or vision, you must identify what specific knowledge and skills you will need to be successful. You will need to develop an action plan to achieve the education required and become committed to it. People in your leadership will be more than happy to help you with this entire process.

By applying the active learner law, you will increase your chances of getting what you want. Certainly, your leaders look for evidence that you have a healthy appetite for learning. More important, they look for evidence that you have an enthusiasm to work effectively with others, can assume responsibility, and have the ability to motivate others to high performance.

Assessing and Addressing Your Basic Deficiencies

People are interested in things you know, can do, and feel. They know that no one person excels in everything, and everyone can improve his or her skills and attitudes. They respect those who have assessed their deficiencies and are doing something to correct the deficiencies. If someone perceives that you have a positive attitude, they will admire you and be more likely to do business with you.

I recently met the "perfect person." The gentleman spent so much time telling me how wonderful he was; he talked me out of associating with him. People who think they are perfect have at least two major problems: (1) they will lie to you, and (2) they will lie to themselves.

Once you have decided on your long-range goal or vision and have developed a plan to reach it, discover your skill deficiencies by matching the skill requirements of the goal to skills and abilities you already possess. Your leadership will be able to help you with this task.

Discovering social or attitudinal deficiencies is more difficult because we are reluctant to tell others about our shortcomings, and most of us are protective of things that affect our self-esteem. An honest review of your social behavior and personal attitudes can be accomplished by conducting an assessment. Ask (or have someone else ask) your peers and family members to evaluate your team building, team playing, communication, and work ethic skills. Some useful personality assessment instruments should be available from your leadership. These personality profiles can be very helpful in identifying behaviors that come naturally and ones that you'll have to work on. A review of past performance evaluations will often provide the information you need to objectively assess your behavioral deficiencies. Sometimes a candid visit with a good friend can be revealing.

In any case, smart people seek to discover their deficiencies and resolve to correct them through a personal development plan that may include books, tapes, seminars, and a conscious effort to change behaviors. You need to identify your deficiencies and work hard to eliminate them, but do not despair about them. You can accomplish almost anything if your desire is strong enough.

Many famous people have overcome serious deficiencies to be among the best in their field. Winston Churchill held the lowest academic rank in his elementary school. General George Patton was dyslexic and flunked mathematics at the U.S. Military Academy. Remember Helen Keller? You get the point.

One final note. Many organizations provide learning opportunities for their people. Take advantage of these opportunities. When your leadership understands you are interested in self-improvement through staff development opportunities, you'll have one more credit on the right side of the ledger.

Advice from the Pros

Bill Dowdell is President of the Flexographic

Technical Association, a highly respected national organization for the flexography (printing) industry. He has worked all over the country with hundreds of employers and offers this insight to the importance of continuous learning: "Learning new skills has two significant and invaluable benefits for the [people and the leadership]: first, it indicates an ability to *continually improve* within the present function that is so important for a company to remain competitive. Second, in today's technical environment, radical changes in manufacturing and service industries demand the incorporation of processes that enable a company to remain in business and compete in a leadership position."

Bill's advice to people who wish to advance is: "Demonstrate the ability to perform the [skills necessary] in the next level of [leadership]. . ."

Gene Rackley, a partner of Heidrick and Struggles, a nationally respected executive search firm, has worked with thousands of corporate executives and thoroughly understands the labor challenges they face. He and his company believe that all outstanding leaders must have a high appetite for knowledge and learning. "More importantly," Gene relates, "they must actively continue improving their knowledge and skills to be peak performers."

Gene gives this advice to people who wish to excel in their business: "Base your life on unshakable values. Be self-motivated, confident, organized, enthusiastic, and develop good interpersonal communication skills. You'll become as influential as possible!"

Allen Tate, owner and CEO of one of America's largest privately owned real estate corporations, believes that successful people never miss an opportunity to improve their skills. He has this advice for people who want to be successful in business: "Get focused on your goal, be enthusiastic in every social context, and recognize that the best way to help yourself is to help others."

Conclusion

Applying the Law of Learning is essential for becoming influential to others. Successful professionals are willing and eager to correct skill deficiencies. Your ability to constantly work toward improvement is important. The goal of this Ninth Law for Becoming Influential is to convince others that you are able to learn new skills and perform in new ways, and that you always have their best interest at heart.

Practical Advice

Discovering new knowledge, new skills, and better social skills is an exciting part of life. As you work your way through this process of self-improvement to optimize your opportunities, remember that learning is truly lifelong. The very business of life should include constant growth.

Points to Ponder

✧ Learn to earn.
✧ Keep your skills current.
✧ Demonstrate your skills.
✧ Assess and address your deficiencies.

From This Day Forward

◆ I will actively engage in professional development activities that will help me reach my career vision.

◆ _____
_____

◆ _____
_____

◆ _____
_____

Conclusion

By applying the Nine Essential Laws for Becoming Influential, you can expect to be successful in life. This will come by reading, understanding, and applying the principles of this book. You have every reason to feel secure with yourself and your ability to achieve your goal. The only true security rests with your belief in yourself, a clear vision, and your ability to apply these nine laws. Once you recognize the truth of this matter, you will be free from the gripping fear of failure. You will also cease being emotionally dependent on your leadership. You will experience a freedom from fear and a release from whatever binds you to an expected condition.

Establishing your vision, developing a consistently positive attitude, obtaining the right skills, and having faith in God and yourself will sustain you through the tough times and ultimately propel you into career success. You can begin now to face your next step with confidence. You obviously have the personal motivation to excel, or you would not have read this entire book in the first place. You can also have confidence in the fact that you have read the right book, know the universal secrets to becoming as influential as possible, and now have the opportunity to put your knowledge to work for you. You have the right stuff.

Best wishes!
Tony Zeiss

Appendix A

Characteristics, Skills, and Behaviors Most Valued by Others

While conducting the research for this book, I asked the people who contributed to list the characteristics, skills, and behaviors what they most valued in employees. I received over thirty different categorical preferences and close to 180 different responses. The following list demonstrates those characteristics, skills, and behaviors most valued:

Positive Attitude
Enthusiasm
Integrity
Tustworthiness
Interpersonal
Communication Skill
Self Motivated
Ambitious
Loyal
Committed
Knowledge and Skills
Flexible
Open Minded
Willing to Change
Team Player
Gets Along With Others
Goal Oriented
Focused
Dependable
Perseveres
Compassionate
Fair
Teachable
Creative

Appendix B

Goal Exercise

The following exercise is the most important in the entire book. Your responses to these five statements will form the core of your plan and will prepare you with the confidence that comes from knowing yourself and what you can do. Use only one sentence for each statement.

1. State your immediate objective.

2. State your long term goal (or where you intend to be ten years from now).

3. State why you have chosen this business.

4. State why you believe you will succeed.

5. State how you can be helpful to others.

The completion of this exercise will result in a five-sentence biography that you can relate in clear language while networking. You could even have this snappy biography printed on your business cards or on the flap of your personalized thank-you notes!

About the Author

Tony Zeiss holds a doctorate in higher education and is a nationally recognized leader in organizational development. His thirty years of experience in higher education have been highlighted by his prominence in education and in the development of people.

He supervised the development of one of the first U.S. Department of Labor approved skills centers, chaired the Colorado State Job Training Coordinating Council, serves on Vice President Gore's Workforce Leadership Group, and led two colleges into national prominence through his focus on America's workforce.

He is a prolific writer and speaker whose previous books include *Economic Development: a Viewpoint of Business, Creating a Literate Society* (with a preface by Barbara Bush), *Community College Leadership in the Twenty-First Century, and The Twelve Essential Laws For Getting A Job.* He is also a popular consultant and professional speaker, and has served on the board for the Zig Ziglar Corporation.

Dr. Zeiss is currently president of Central Piedmont Community College, which serves 70,000 students each year in Charlotte, North Carolina.